Living With An Angel

Ruth Ann

Living With An Angel
by Ruth Ann
Copyright © 2019 by Ruth Ann
First published October 2019

ISBN 978-0-578-59356-2

Printed by Amazon. Published by KHC Angel Books. PO Box 241, Hayden, ID 83835-9998

Direct inquiries to the address above. All rights reserved by Ruth Ann and KHC Angel Books. Except for use in review, no portion of this book may be reproduced in any form without the express written permission of the publisher.

Edited by Jennifer Supp
Cover art by Stephanie Hannus

DEDICATION

This book is dedicated to all of the angels that are living or have lived here on earth and touched the lives of so many.

CONTENTS

	Introduction	vii
	Quotes	xi
Chapter One	Jutona's Chapter	Pg 1
Chapter Two	David's Chapter	Pg 13
Chapter Three	Chase's Chapter	Pg 23
Chapter Four	Mark's Chapter	Pg 33
Chapter Five	Maria's Chapter	Pg 43
Chapter Six	Joshua's Chapter	Pg 49
Chapter Seven	Jenifer's Chapter	Pg 53
Chapter Eight	Matthew's Chapter	Pg 59
	Epilogue	Pg 71
	Acknowledgements	Pg 73

Introduction

I believe in my heart that every being on earth has a purpose or reason for existing. The reasons for their existence are as great as the number of individuals. People and experiences continually come into and out of our lives providing us with opportunities for personal growth and a multitude of choices that are as individual as we are. Yet there are some among us who may not have had a choice in how they have been able to physically live their life but, are here on earth or in our hearts to provide love, lessons, and support for those who may desperately need it. These individuals I refer to as "Angels".

Most of the Angels in this book never became adults but, spread their messages as children to whoever would listen. The unique spirit of each Angel remains with us at all times. Through my life experiences I have had the opportunity to become acquainted with a variety of children with varying abilities and their families. I do not think that I was ever surprised however, I have been amazed or in awe of the resiliency of not only the children but of their friends, caretakers, educators, and family members as well.

Watching a child live their life within any confines let alone the confines that may be dictated by illness, condition, or syndrome can be very difficult for all those concerned. In my experiences I have had the distinct pleasure to meet with many families and friends of children with varying abilities who are most thankful that they had the opportunity to not only to know and love their child but to learn from them as well.

The image of Angels living among us can lead to thoughts of heavenly beings rather than to earthly beings or those existing in our hearts. The children realized in this book actually lived or are currently living and spreading their love, laughter, and lessons. All we have to do is open out hearts, listen, and learn.

While interviewing concerned adults, there have been several occasions when the children have been referred to as "our Angel", "the Angel who saved our family", or "My personal Angel". These heartfelt references are used when conveying the unconditional love, appreciation, and lessons learned from the beautiful Angels brought into the lives of others. This book will be relaying information which will hopefully describe the impact that children are able to make in the lives of others when hearts are opened.

All of the Angels described in this book are very brave souls who have not allowed their illness, condition, or syndrome to define who they are or place limits on their accomplishments.

Every person who contributed to this book had a deep love, respect, and affection for their "Angel".

* The characters and situations in this book are based on true life stories. In some instances, names of the characters have been changed to protect privacy.

Quotes

In researching quotes, sayings or opinions from others on Angels, I found an overabundance available from many sources. This finding was very eye-opening for me as until the thought of writing this book, I had never thought of developing a complete thought or opinion on what an angel is or what they actually do, or what their purpose may be to others.

There are "Angel" quotes dispersed throughout the book. These are a compilation of quotes from a variety of people which are meant to be thought provoking and may help us determine how Angels impact the lives of ourselves as well as others.

This first poem causes a reflection on a particular family that I had the pleasure of getting to know.

We, unaccustomed to courage
exiles from delight
live coiled in shells of loneliness
until love leaves its high holy temple
and comes into our sight
to liberate us into life.

Love arrives
and in its train come ecstasies
old memories of pleasure
ancient histories of pain.
Yet, if we are bold, love strikes away the chains of fear
from our souls.

We are weaned from our timidity
In the flush of love's light
we dare be brave
And suddenly we see
that love costs all we are
and will ever be.
Yet it is only love
which sets us free.

Maya Angelo

Chapter One
Jutona's Chapter
January 10, 2003/August 24, 2012

"Those we love don't go away,
They walk beside us every day,
Unseen, unheard, but always near,
Still loved, still missed, and very dear."

Unknown

    Jutona is a beautiful Angel who was born on January 10, 2003. She was born into a family which included her mother, an older brother and older sister. Jutona's birth mother was addicted to methamphetamines and was actively partaking in substances throughout all of her pregnancies. All of the biological siblings demonstrate to varying degrees behaviors associated with drug exposure in utero.

Jutona's adoptive mother, Pennie, has reported that Jutona's biological mother passed away in 2004 of a brain tumor (glioblastoma multiforme) shortly after giving birth to Jutona's younger sister. Jutona's great great Aunt and great great Uncle also passed away of the same type of brain tumor. The brain tumor that ultimately took Jutona's life is considered to have been a genetic issue.

Jutona was born addicted to methamphetamines however, the greater challenge that Jutona would face in her short life was perhaps the genetic issue. Jutona's biological mother passed away while in her 20's of a brain tumor (glioblastoma multiforme) when Jutona was around 11 months old. This same type of brain tumor would also claim Jutona's life. The brain tumor for both mother and daughter was a rarity in itself considering their ages. *This particular brain tumor usually occurs in people over 50 years of age and rarely in those under 30 years of age. After a courageous battle for about 4 years from her original diagnosis, Jutona also passed away from the effects of the same type brain tumor. She never gave up; she never lost her spark.

I will always remember the first time that I met Jutona. She had already had treatment for her tumor after the original diagnosis of glioblastoma multiforme which occurred when she was in Kindergarten. Despite this discovery and treatment at such an early age, her smiles lit up the room. Her curiosity was contagious. She was always ready to help others, adults and children, family, friends, and strangers alike. Her desire to blend in and be just like all of the other children was admirable and, I might add on this point, she was very determined. During this first meeting Pennie appeared exhausted however, she was all business and seriously and completely dedicated to making Jutona's life the best it could possibly be.

To better understand the impact that this tumor had on her life the following is the definition of glioblastoma multiforme according to Columbia Neurosurgery.

"Glioblastoma Multiforme is a malignant tumor of the brain. This is one type of a group of tumors collectively known as astrocytomas - so called because they originate from astrocyte cells -." These tumors are most aggressive and the most common type of tumor which starts in the brain. They are most often found in the cerebrum.

Symptoms associated with Glioblastoma Multiforme were found on webmd.com. Because glioblastomas grow quickly, pressure on the brain usually causes the first symptoms. Depending on where the tumor is, it can cause:

constant headaches

seizures

vomiting

difficulty thinking

mood changes

double or blurred vision

difficulty speaking

Following Jutona's biological mother's death, a long and tedious custody battle for the four children had ensued. The conflict was between other family members and Pennie, Jutona's mother's aunt. Pennie and her husband Jim were ultimately able to adopt all four of the children. Jutona and her three siblings were adopted in November of 2005 by Pennie and Jim. Pennie is sister to Jutona's grandfather. All four of the children in Jutona's family were accepted and adopted into the aunt's already established family. Jutona was two years old at the time of the adoption. Her new family included Pennie and her husband, two grown children from her husband's prior marriage, two grown children from Pennie's prior marriage, and two children from her marriage with her current husband, Jim. Pennie and Jim are now known and referred to as "mom and dad" by all of the children adopted from Jutona's biological mother. (For the rest of this chapter the terms "mom" and "dad" will be used in reference to Jutona's adoptive parents.)

    Jutona was 5 years old and two weeks into her Kindergarten year of public school when her tumor was originally discovered. Her treatment was very aggressive as this type of tumor is difficult to treat and cure. She underwent stem cell treatment therapy to help her young body recover from the more aggressive cancer treatment, as this type of tumor is difficult to treat and cure. She was told how hard this treatment would be and how sick she would be during this treatment. As was usual, Jutona tried to be happy however, the treatment was constant and relentless taking its toll on her small body. She was constantly throwing up, in pain, and in intensive care for three weeks. At one point her heart rate went up to over 200 and her kidneys began to shut down. Angel Jutona did persevere. She did beat the cancer demon this time. Once Jutona had completed this treatment she did get better and her smiles returned, much to her relief and the relief of her family and friends.

During Jutona's recovery from initial treatment the professionals working with her from the hospital where she was being treated were very concerned for her safety. The school staff, administrators, and classroom teacher were quite concerned as well. Jutona wanted to be just like the other kids and be allowed to do all of the things her peers were able to do. Jutona's mom was very supportive of her being allowed to live her life as a typical and inquisitive little girl. Her mother supported Jutona's decision to be like all of her friends and had the school lift all of the restrictions in place for Jutona except the universal precautions that were in place to keep all of the students safe. As she recovered from her treatment, she was able to attend school in the least restrictive environment possible. She thoroughly enjoyed being with her friends.

Angel Jutona's effects on those around her was nothing short of amazing whether at school, at home, or out and about in the community. Whenever she was home she brought much joy to the entire family with each member being positively impacted, depending on the relationship they had with Jutona. The home was much calmer and peaceful when Jutona was present. One friend who also had a child undergoing treatment in the hospital at the same time as Jutona's 1st round of treatment, volunteered to help take care of Jutona saying that Jutona's voice was very captivating, soothing, and appreciated. The Pastor of the church where the family were members, said that Jutona was an inspiration to the entire congregation as she was always happy no matter how ill she was.

It is very difficult for family members and friends to understand and come to terms with the fact that a loved one is experiencing a terminal illness. The changes in physical appearance, behaviors, and mannerisms in the one afflicted are so very hard to accept. Many times, family and friends can have the feelings of being inadequate, alone, or lost as they try to deal with watching their loved one suffer. Sometimes helping to care for their loved one during this process is simply more than they are capable of. Watching a child (or anyone) who is virtually terminally ill can cause the people who are the caretakers feel inadequate and helpless as they watch their loved one become weaker and weaker.

When Jutona was originally diagnosed with glioblastoma multiforme, her Grandfather, biological mother's father, went into a significant depression which was understandable as he had watched as his daughter had passed away from the same illness just a few years prior. When Jutona was diagnosed the second time, her grandfather was absolutely devastated.

During the course of my interview with Pennie she had stated that she was usually alone with Jutona during hospital stays. Pennie was asked why several of the other members of the family had not come to visit Jutona while she was so very ill and in the hospital. Pennie's reply was carefully considered in respect to each of the immediate family members. She answered that it seemed Jutona's sisters were really too young to understand the gravity of the situation. Jutona's older brother, who was eleven years old at the time of this second round of treatment and had served as the caretaker for her and all of his younger sisters when their biological mother was alive, appeared to be afraid for her and could not bear to see her sick. Jim also could not bear to see her sick and in the hospital with such a serious illness where he was helpless to ease her pain.

At each and every turn of Jutona's treatment her mother was there for her. Pennie spent countless days and nights away from the rest of the family so she could be with Jutona wherever she was and for as long as her treatment was given. They were able to spend much time together talking about her illness, treatment and eventually what the outcome would be for Jutona. Pennie is able to recall all of her moments with Jutona be they good, difficult, and sad and retold this particular story. It appears that the second time that Jutona was diagnosed and the day before she was to undergo surgery, Jutona was told that her tumor had returned. She asked her mom, "Why me and not the other girls?" (referring to her sisters). Her mother told her, "Because you can handle it." Jutona agreed!

One story that Pennie shared was recalling an occasion when Jutona had come home after her initial treatment. The family had gone out to dinner at a family restaurant. Jutona had lost her hair as a result of her treatment and was wearing a hat. She was amazed by an older couple in the restaurant who kept looking at her. She was not alarmed, she was not afraid, nor was she angry or confused. On her way out of the restaurant as she passed the table where the couple were seated, Jutona simply took off her hat and told them that she had cancer and then walked on. This message was from a child who was 5 years old at the time. She passed no judgment, nor did she speak unkind words. Perhaps many of us could learn a lesson in kindness, understanding, and wisdom from this Angel.

The second time that the tumor was discovered, Jutona was in the Second Grade. This time around she kept up her smiles and positive attitude through all of the treatments provided to her. This time she did not get better. This time Angel Jutona did not go home to her family and all those who loved her so very much. Our very brave Angel Jutona passed away at 9 years old with more wisdom, kindness, and courage than many of us accomplish in a lifetime.

Throughout all of the multitude of treatments, stays in the hospital, and therapy sessions Jutona maintained her patience with all of her health issues and those who wanted to make her life as comfortable as possible. She wanted to be like a regular kid. She did not want the over-protectiveness or the comments and looks of pity.

    Angel Jutona led a very courageous battle against cancer as well as with society in order to be able to live her short life as normally as possible. She left behind the gift of wisdom, demonstration of how to be kind to one another, and how understanding others actions can prevent anger and frustration. She showed us how happiness can be found for all of us. Jutona is one very unforgettable Angel!
* - UCLA.edu -neurosurgery

"Life is full of moments that only you and your angel share."

Anonymous

Chapter Two
David's Chapter

"The golden moments in the stream of life rush past us, and we see nothing but sand; the angels come to visit us, and we only know them when they are gone."

George Eliot (George Eliot is a pen name for Mary Anne Evans. During the Victorian era she was a journalist, poet, novelist, and translator.)

David is a beautiful and talented child with many medical and health issues who lives with his parents in a single-family home. He has an older brother of an adult age who is estranged and not allowed to come to the home. Therefore, David is virtually an only child. David is 13 years old and, just like all other teens, wants to be like everyone else. The issue is that, in reality, he will never have the opportunity to behave as his more typically developing peers.

David was born with Cystic Fibrosis which is "a hereditary disorder affecting the exocrine glands. It causes the production of abnormally thick mucus, leading to the blockage of the pancreatic ducts, intestines, and bronchi and often resulting in respiratory infection." (1)(taken from the web dictionary). Although the life expectancy of individuals with Cystic Fibrosis varies, it is known that the disease does cut short the life of those inflicted. This disease used to be fatal with the average life expectancy in the 20"s. Now many of those afflicted are living to be between 42 and 45 years of age. Sometimes the treatment (pounding on the patient's back) may be worse than the disease itself. There also are possible secondary effects such as pneumonia that put the patient further at risk for becoming a fatality. It is unknown how long he may live, but David isn't concerned with that fact. He lives each day learning as much as he can, not allowing the question of his longevity to make an impact.

David's parents not only have their concerns for him and his longevity and quality of life but, have their own personal struggles while they continue to give David as much support as they are able. Every person has their coping mechanisms. Some mechanisms are more functional than others. I do not believe that any one person is able to put themselves into another's life and say, "You could have handled it this way." No two people have the same experience, history, knowledge, support systems, or personality. These qualities make comparisons virtually impossible of a person's abilities to cope with strenuous situations.

Most of us are aware of the effects that stress may have on our bodies, emotions, and attitudes. Although no one can ever be certain of the origin of conditions, David's mother has developed migraine headaches and is chronically ill. She has become obese and though she has had gastric bypass surgery, she is currently medicated and continues to be overweight. David's father is working two jobs to help keep up with the ever-accumulating pile of medical bills however, remains a very pleasant person to interact with. When we look at children that have potentially challenging abilities, we may or may not always see the invisible or underlying issues that the parents are dealing with on a daily basis. Both parents love David very much and are trying to the best of their ability to understand and cope with David's illness and the impact it has on family dynamics. Some of the factors which are affecting David's parents are: the need for a greater support system, the relationship with David's estranged half-brother, depression, personal health issues, poverty, exhaustion, and their own isolation due to the constant care required for David. So many precautions must be taken to protect David's health; face masks must be worn by all those who enter the home. There are even house cleaners that are specialized in caring for the environment of people such as David.

    Cystic Fibrosis is a disease which causes David to constantly be on an IV (intravenous flow). In addition, he is still a frequent patient in the hospital. His medical fragility frequently places him in isolation and limits his ability to interact with peers which in turn affects his strong desire to "be like everyone else". As stated above, David is also quite intelligent and naturally inquisitive. However, David's medical issues are not what are focused on by his homebound teacher. An exceptional education teacher is allowed to come into David's home for 4 hours/week which greatly limits his time for his academic program. State funding allows for each student that receives services as a homebound student a maximum of 4 hours/week.

In a perfect or ideal life, all children would be allowed to grow and develop with absolute freedom from limitations placed on them. I happen to be a believer that an ideal life is only possible when it includes diversity of individuals, challenges, and experiences.

David is a very bright and inquisitive child as well as an excellent student. He has a wonderful sense of humor and is very witty. He is scheduled to attend school in a classroom for three hours each week however, all too often he misses this opportunity due to illness or hospitalizations. The act of attending school with peers is in itself a threat to David as his illness puts him at great risk for contracting or developing infections. When he is well enough to attend class in the classroom he enjoys interacting with his peers and participation on the swim team.

While peers are a very important and valued part of David's life, he does have limited exposure to relationships outside of the home. David was very excited to have an opportunity to travel to Asia to visit with an exchange student he had become acquainted with over the past year. Before the trip David contracted an infection and it was questionable if he would be well enough to travel. Fortunately, this time he overcame the illness in time to take his trip. There is another student that he particularly enjoys playing chess with. He seems to be liked and accepted by his peers. Like many others, he likes to control the interactions he has with others which can cause some hard feelings. It makes sense that he likes to control his interactions with others as so much of his life is controlled for him. David has limited freedom or opportunity to make choices of his own.

    I had an opportunity to speak with David's homebound exceptional education teacher, Melissa*. I found the perspective of the teacher to be somewhat different than the perspective coming from a parent. This difference in perspective is as it should be. During the interview, Melissa described him as being very bright. He loves the water and wants to become an Oceanographer. Although David is technically in the 9th grade he has a high IQ and is reading at an advanced grade level, has splinter skills in math, and is generally an advanced learner.

    Melissa shared that David has high expectations for himself. He scores high on his most of his tests and progress monitoring. Progress monitoring is a method of demonstrating his ability to continue to make significant progress academically. His expectations are to know everything and when there is something that he does not know, he will get a negative attitude. (This is a behavior that appears to be typical to that of many children his age!)

    Melissa did comment that she is able to tell if he is in a bad mood, which is a rare occasion occurrence. Typically, he wants to learn and does not want to cut his learning time short. Learning is a privilege and reward to David. He very much looks forward to his weekly sessions with his in-home teacher. I think that the teacher Melissa best describes her relationship with David when she said that they learn and laugh together. David is also allowed to conduct research for himself so that he might challenge Melissa. This makes for a fun exchange, lots of bantering, and a great deal of learning in a short time!

    David is a student and person who is very much admired by others. He is admired not just for his courage to stand up to all of the medical challenges that he faces, but for his positive attitude that is constantly displayed. During one of the infrequent times that David was in the classroom, another student asked him how he was able to function without complaining. David replied, "I look around me and see others worse off, how can I complain."

David has been on and continues to be on an arduous life's journey. His resilience is typical of that found in all people who choose to face challenges with gusto. Each time he faces a challenge (which is usually medical), David approaches these difficulties without complaining. Even when he is in the hospital or receiving treatments at home, there is NO COMPLAINING from David. That behavior in itself is to be commended as many people spend quite a bit of their daily life
complaining about one thing or another.

David wants to learn and progress. He has often become the teacher in his quest to learn. He has pushed his teacher to learn about many things outside of her knowledge by frequently asking many questions and creating various scenarios. Melissa is often required to do additional research to learn about topics that David may demonstrate having an interest in just to keep up with his curiosity. For example, during the lesson of the day (CNN 10 is a favorite show for him to watch and is incorporated into his learning plan) David may ask a question about a topic that comes up and is not addressed in his regular curriculum. Melissa takes advantage of these "teaching moments" and will delve into the subject and return with answers and explanations until David is satisfied and ready to move on to another topic for discussion.

When I asked Melissa to reflect on what she thought David has taught her or given to her, she replied, "To live life positively, not to be self-centered and never complain. If I have not learned something from David, I have missed the boat." Sometimes with adults, parents, teachers, friends, and relative's interactions with others are about their needs rather than focusing on one who is suffering. There are very high expectations placed on David because when he feels well his attitude makes it difficult to tell that his health and life are compromised. Educational expectations placed on him by others as well as day to day life expectations can become unrealistic.

As of this printing Angel David is here on earth with us right now. He gives the great gift of himself to us every day to cherish and enjoy. This wonderful person is a child who has demonstrated how resiliency and perseverance has been able to afford him happiness in the life he has been given. He is teaching us to be grateful for what we have and to be accepting of ourselves. He is teaching us how to become better people by learning and laughing and he shows us that there is grace in diversity. David will always be remembered as a bright light in the lives of all who have had the privilege of knowing him.

"Angels live among us. Sometimes they hide their wings, but there is no disguising the peace and hope they bring."

Unknown

Chapter Three
Chase's Chapter

"I don't see how I possibly could have come from where I entered the planet to where I am now if there had not been angels along the way."

Della Reese (Della was an actress, singer, and ordained minister. One role she is remembered for is the TV series "Touched by an Angel".)

Chase Galloway is a beautiful angel who was born on September 15, 2010. He was born with a condition noted as holoprosencephaly. He currently is living with a very loving family that has adopted him.

The Galloway Family fell in love with him almost immediately as do most of the people who are fortunate enough to encounter him.

I met Chase when he was three years old and transitioning into public school from Early Intervention services. I had already met his adopted mother, Kelli, as our school district had previously enrolled one of her foster children. When we had our transition meeting and Chase entered the room with his mother pushing him in a stroller, there came with him an air of calm that I will never forget. At that point I had worked for 28 years with children of varying abilities and had never experienced anything like it (and I never have since). I sat in awe of this experience and had difficulty completing the mountains of paperwork required as we continued with our meeting, setting goals, discussing services, and how the services would be delivered based on Chase's needs.

Chase's biological mother, Jesse, suffers from mental illness and is a drug addict as well. It is believed she had sought an abortion to end the pregnancy and had taken a great deal of additional drugs in an attempt to abort. One of the drugs that Jesse was taking was a prescription for lithium due to behaviors associated with Bipolar Disorder.

According to WebMD, "Lithium can poison a developing fetus and can increase the risk of birth defects, including heart problems." Wikipedia - There is a correlation between holoprosencephaly and the use of various drugs including lithium. Apparently when a woman is taking this medication, it is recommended that she not become pregnant due to the possibility of the baby being born with any of a variety of birth defects.

Holoprosencephaly is a birth defect effecting the development of the face and in brain structure and function. Chase has been diagnosed with holoprosencephaly where the forebrain of the embryo fails to develop into two hemispheres (Wikipedia). The National Institute of Health adds that the failure of the embryonic forebrain to divide into the double lobes results in a single lobed brain structure and severe skull and facial defects. Jesse had no prenatal care which is more than unfortunate, it is a travesty in the case of Chase Galloway.

Labor resulted in a natural delivery of Angel Chase. Jesse had been given a sonogram during labor where it was detected that Chase had holoprosencephaly. According to rarediseases.info.nih the life expectancy with this type of birth defect can be from stillborn to 12 months. At the writing of this book Chase is six years old. It has been explored that, had the mother been under prenatal care, this condition could have been treated in utero. Of course, there is no crystal ball that can tell us if the treatment would have cured or lessened the effects of holoprosencephaly, however I believe that we can all agree that good prenatal care is always an advantage to both the mother and the fetus. Kelli concludes that there could have been a different outcome for Chase had he been able to receive prenatal care and the early detection of the defect. Perhaps with treatment prior to birth the effects from holoprosencephaly could have prevented or lessened.

According to Wikipedia one of the effects that can go along with the condition of holopropsencephaly is that of epilepsy or seizure disorder with the highest risk of developing seizures being before two years of age. Chase did indeed develop a significant seizure disorder that at times has been very difficult to get under control. The seizures have now been under control, for the most part, for the last two years. In addition to holoprosencephaly and seizures, Chase is diagnosed with Cerebral Palsy.

After Chase was born, his biological mother did agree to have a shunt implanted to drain fluid from the brain. Everyone at the hospital was concerned for his ability to survive. Chase was placed in a hospital rehabilitation facility after he was born and had the shunt implanted. The Galloway family had previously been identified as the foster family for Chase. At one point staff at the rehabilitation facility had told Kelli that Chase had died! This, of course was not an accurate account of his state at the time.

During his stay in the hospital rehabilitation area, it had been discovered that Chase was actually a very special child. He was described as being a child with "Super Powers". At an early age Chase demonstrated that he indeed had the power to mesmerize those around him. This story came as no surprise to me as I have stated how I was affected the first time we met.

For the two months that Chase was hospitalized, he had no parent advocate assigned to him. The Galloway Family could not make recommendations or any decisions regarding Chase's treatment until they were actually handed legal custody of the baby. All decisions were being made by the medical staff. Adoptive mother, Kelli

Galloway, reported this as being a very frustrating experience. Kelli knew that Chase had many needs and was more than willing to advocate for him during his hospital stay. Chase was finally discharged to the care of the Galloway family when he was two months old. At the time of discharge, the Galloway family consisted of Father and Mother, 3 boys who were born to the couple, 3 adopted girls, and 2 adopted boys. Chase was welcomed into the family by all members with open arms!

    The Galloway family is no stranger to living with others demonstrating varying abilities. Kelli had been the caretaker of her uncle who was born with Down Syndrome. The spectrum of effects for this disorder ranges from mild to severe. Kelli's uncle's effects from this syndrome were quite serious which helped to give her some experience in caring for an individual with medical, physical, and cognitive difficulties.

    Regardless, the family willingly accepted Chase into their loving arms. Over the years there have been quite a few other foster children placed in the Galloway home with several demonstrating difficult behaviors. Kelli reports that there have been alone over 20 newborn infants placed with her family. Many of the foster children were placed for a short time but several have had an "extended stay".

Chase is considered an overwhelming gift from God to the family. He brought with him into the home a wave of love. When Chase was sent to live with the Galloways, he was sent with cautions that were to prepare the family for his death. It was indicated to them that he did not have enough brain development to live. Chase not only continued to thrive but, continues to grow stronger. His progress can be considered "up & down" but he never gives up. The biological mother's rights were severed when Chase was 8 months old and the adoption into the Galloway family completed when he was about 18 months old.

Chase brought with him into the home a wonderful sense of humor. Sometimes he will laugh just before a situation is amusing and sometimes, he will laugh with another member of the family. He really has no vision to see what is so humorous, but one can't help but notice his smile that seems to come from his heart. Chase is typically a happy child and he can become typically fussy or cry when he is unhappy or if he is not feeling well. For instance, he was a little out of sorts when his hip was pulled out of place and he had a plate and pins installed for 5 weeks while it healed.

As stated earlier, the Galloway family has many members, but they also have many friends and a large circle of those who offer their support. Kelli said she could not care for all of the children that she does if she did not have support from others. One of the greatest support networks for the family is their church. When Chase first began attending church, the sounds were too loud for him and he cried. He generally sat out in the foyer with his mother. Other members of the congregation (Chase's "Church Family") would stop by to see them, have a visit, or offer a greeting after the church services. Eventually the church added on a "Cry Room" especially for Chase and his mom. He and other children are now able to attend church without becoming overwhelmed.

Chase has many times been admitted to the hospital for one reason or another as a result of his medical conditions. His "Church Family" will often come to visit him in the hospital and at home. Mother says that they are under the influence of Chase's "Super Powers". This special "Church Family" offers support and prayers for Chase and his family. Like many other people, they have fallen in love with him.

When I asked Kelli how Chase impacts the other members of the Galloway family, she responded that Chase has changed all of those who have met him or just been close to him in more ways than we may ever realize. He has taught those around him how to be kind, how to love unconditionally, he has brought people together, and he has demonstrated that it is possible to meet and/or exceed the expectations that others have placed on you.

Chase defeated the prognosis that was given to him at the beginning of his life. He has helped to show others to allow more hope into their lives. When the Galloway family received Chase as a foster child, they were given only the downside of the expectations if he were to live. Kelli wished that the medical staff could have been a little more positive and described what his life could be like if he did survive.

The accomplishments that Chase has gathered since his birth are many and miraculous. The number of lives he has touched and impacted are more than most of us will experience in our entire lives.

Chase's mother has expressed herself in a way only a loving mother is able. Kelli feels that the Lord has given her many opportunities to experience the impact and motivation that her Angels have given her over the years. The impact that Angel Chase has placed on myself as well as hundreds of others cannot possibly be measured. I will cherish his gifts forever.

"Angels aren't in heaven...
They are on earth...
But not everyone is able to see them."

Unknown

Chapter Four
Mark's Chapter

"Everything happens for a reason, even if we are not wise enough to see it."

Oprah Winfrey (Oprah is one of my heroines whose wisdom, kindness, and generosity has touched the lives of millions of people.)

"People are in your life for a reason, season, or lifetime."

Oprah Winfrey

Mark is an angel who is now 45 years old and was brought to us on August 9th, 1973. Mark was born with Down syndrome, so before I tell you about our beautiful Angel Mark, I will give some information to help better understand Down syndrome.

I had typically looked at children with Down syndrome as being placed educationally into categories depending on their level of cognitive functioning. I also was fortunate enough early on to determine that first and foremost these children are to be treated as individuals.

Clinically, there are three categories of Down syndrome. The chances per category appears to depend on the type of chromosome rearrangement and which chromosomes are involved. According to the National Association for Down Syndrome (www.nads.org), Down syndrome is defined as a genetic chromosome 21 disorder that impacts physical and intellectual development. "It occurs in 1 in every 792 live births. Individuals with Down syndrome have 47 chromosomes instead of the usual 46." "It is the most frequently occurring chromosomal disorder."

The Down Syndrome Association of Central Ohio (dsaco.net) describes the three categories of Down syndrome as follows:

Trisomy 21 (nondisjunction) - The most common occurring at 95%. This occurs when there are 3 rather than 2 #21 chromosomes present in every cell of the body.

Translocation - This occurs when part of chromosome #21 breaks off during cell division and attaches to another chromosome, typically from chromosome #14. Translocation occurs in 4% of individuals.

Mosaicism - The occurs when the non-disjunction of chromosome #21 takes place in one - but not all - of the initial cell divisions after fertilization. When this occurs, there is a mixture of 2 types of cells. Mosaicism occurs in 1% of individuals with Down syndrome.

An additional definition for Down syndrome is from an organization called Lifespan in conjunction with Rhode Island Hospital. (www.lifespan.org). "Down syndrome is a genetic disorder. It is also called trisomy 21. It includes certain birth defects, learning problems, and facial features. A child with Down syndrome may also have heart defects and problems with vision and hearing. How severe these problems are varies from child to child."

Down syndrome individuals have an average life expectancy of 60 years. This is a significant increase from the average expectancy of 25 years in 1983. This increase in life expectancy has been attributed to the end of institutionalizing of individuals with Down syndrome. Another factor is likely the increase in medical knowledge.

Mark - Mark was born on August 9, 1973. He is currently 45 years old. Mark's biological mother, Stephanie*, was 18 years old when she became pregnant. She had graduated from high school and was to begin college. Stephanie was the youngest of 10 children. Her parents who were in their 60's at the time, were very upset with her for becoming pregnant and forbid her to keep the baby. An arrangement for adoption upon the birth of the baby was made through a local adoption agency.

It was discovered during the birth of the baby that Down syndrome was suspected. Soon after his birth baby Mark was moved to another hospital where it was confirmed that he did have Down syndrome. The young mother was told not to look at her baby as that would be very devastating to her. When Mark was diagnosed with Down syndrome, the prospective parents backed out of the agreement.

Mark was placed with Child Protective Services and was deemed eligible for foster care. The family where he was ultimately placed for foster care had already been approved prior to Mark's birth so there were no complications with the placement custody. The family had requested a baby under 1 year old. The foster family accepted Mark for who he was and he was entrusted into to the family's care when he was 2 weeks old.

Stephanie began visiting him in the foster home when Mark was about 1 month old. In addition, his grandmother and aunt would come to visit every 2-3 months at the home of the foster family. When Mark was turning 1 year old the three visitors came to celebrate his first birthday.

Mark's Grandfather, who had never visited or set eyes on Mark, had been ill and was in the hospital. After the birthday party the grandmother had gone to the hospital and proceeded to commit suicide. It is suspected by family members that she was unable to cope with the decisions that had been made concerning their daughters' pregnancy and the birth of Mark and was distraught over her and her husband's treatment of their daughter and grandson.

Stephanie asked the foster mother, Jean, to adopt Mark. Stephanie cared very much for her baby.

She recognized that she was unable to care for him financially, emotionally, and physically. Mark would soon be turning two years old and the mother's rights were to be severed. She wanted to make sure that he was permanently placed in his current loving and caring foster home. She had stated that God wanted Jean, the foster mother, to be Mark's mother. She said that he was happy with her and would have siblings.

The Foster parents, Jean and her husband Ed and Stephanie contacted the County Attorney's office to begin the proceedings for a private adoption. They had all gone to the County Attorney's office together. The waiting period for the adoption was to be 1 year after filing the required paperwork. After the filing was initiated, all they had to do was wait. The adoption was finalized just before Mark's 3rd birthday.

When Mark officially joined the family just after his birth, the family members included Dad (Ed), Mom (Jean), Chris 2 years, and Andrea 7 months. When Mark was 13 months old they added Amy. Just before he turned 4 years Allison was born. Lastly, Michael was born before Mark was 5 years old. Wow! There were six children all under the age of 8 years.

Jean told of a visit to the pediatrician before Mark was to be adopted. The doctor, who happened to be a pediatric cardiologist, told Jean that he did not recommend the adoption as Down syndrome children may develop heart issues. Jean told him that he had been caring for Mark since he had been placed in their home as a foster child. She asked if there was any cause to indicate that Mark would develop a heart issue. The doctor told her "No". Jean switched pediatricians.

Mark has always been given the same expectations as his siblings. He attended public school. He was mainstreamed and graduated high school. He was given accommodations in school and at home when necessary. Mark has maintained his health over the years and continues to do so under the loving supervision of his legal guardians, sisters Amy and Allison. He has a healthy diet and gets plenty of exercise.

For all of his life Mark has been watched over by his siblings. His brothers and sisters would actually choose their friends based on how well they accepted and treated Mark. His sisters would all act as the "little mothers" to him. I believe that this protectiveness or "mothering" continues in Mark's adult life.

Mark's parents and siblings knew that he would need care and supervision throughout his life. His parents recognized that there would come a time when they could not keep up with his needs. Guardianship was given to two of his sisters who welcomed him with open arms. The sisters have two very different households and lifestyles and Mark flourishes in both worlds. Although legal guardianship remains with two of his sisters, all of Mark's siblings are actively involved in Mark's life.

One of his sisters who has guardianship, Allison, lives in Tennessee with her family. She has 6 children with the oldest being 19 years old. The family lives on a ten-acre farm which comes complete with farm animals and chores just like any other farm. All of the children are expected to help out and have their chores including Mark.

Mark very much enjoys the time he spends with Allison's family. He really likes to "hang out" with his 19 year-old nephew, Jake. Jake takes Mark out for a drive every now and again. Mark's mother, Jean, also lives in Tennessee near to Allison's farm. She often attends church with the family and enjoys singing with Mark. (Mark is not a gifted singer so not everyone will agree to sing with him.)

Amy shares guardianship over Mark with her sister. She is a business owner with her husband and lives in Arizona. When Mark visits with them he is very involved with Special Olympics. His favorite events are bowling and bocce ball. Amy and her husband Jim are the coaches for Mark's team sports. Mark also has a respite worker who takes him out 1 time a week with a group. Mark has been participating in these outings as for the past 20 years (since he was a young adult). He has had the same respite worker as well.

Whether he is with Amy or Ally, Mark attends many community functions including church and Special Olympics, as well as running errands, going to restaurants, shopping, and many other activities. In Arizona he is on a list to be invited to fundraisers that are conducted by the police and/or Pima County Sheriff's Department. In February of 2018 Mark attended his first prom through the Tim Tebow Foundation Shine. This is all just a part of who Mark has become and how he affects and inspires those around him every day.

Mark has given his family, friends, acquaintances, and all those who encounter him many moments of humor and happiness. He demonstrates a level of determination that is admired by all who know him.

"Stories about angels remind us that we each have something to do a role to play, a calling, and there's no need to have any fear about jumping in and doing it."

Rob Bell (Rob Bell is an American author, former pastor and speaker.)

Chapter Five
Maria's Chapter

"It is impossible to see the angel unless you first have a notion of it."

James Hillman

Maria is an angel who lives at home with her loving family. She has lived with medical issues for much of her life. One of the medical issues impacting Maria's life is diabetes. These issues have impacted not only her life in general but her education as well. She is currently a senior in high school preparing to graduate in December of 2019. Her actual graduation date with her peers should have been in May of 2019 however she was not able to participate.

The family always shows support when it comes to medical issues however educationally there is little support in the home. Many times, this is true for children who are medically fragile as the main goal would be to keep them alive and as well as can be expected.

Maria has had the same special education teacher in and out of her life since she was in the fifth grade. The homebound teacher, Miss Sandy, has agreed to continue with Maria until she graduates. (Miss Sandy is a special educator who travels to her students whether they are at home or in a hospital setting.) In an interview with Miss Sandy she recalls several incidents in Maria's young life.

Maria first met Miss Sandy when she was in the fifth grade and placed on a Section 504 Plan to have educational accommodations available to her. About a year and a half ago Maria suffered a stroke which landed her in the hospital for 2 weeks. The stroke has left Maria blind in one eye. In addition to her regular schoolwork she was trying to recover from the impact of the stroke. During this time, she was receiving her education at home from Miss Sandy. Maria's school district failed her in all of her subjects for that semester which is when she became half a year behind her peers.

The impact from Maria's stroke led the school district to conduct an initial evaluation to determine eligibility for special education services. She was found to qualify under the category of Other Health Impaired. Her IEP stated that she was to be placed back in the classroom and therefore would not have Miss Sandy as her teacher any longer. Maria became over stressed and overwhelmed with trying to keep up in the school environment and experienced migraine headaches. She returned to the hospital with a serious illness. Miss Sandy returned as her teacher.

Maria is currently taking massive amounts of medications and is on steroids. She is reading at the eighth-grade level and her math is at a basic level. Due to her illnesses she has missed a great deal of instruction which as stated earlier has pushed back her graduation date. Maria also wanted to attend her Senior prom. She had purchased a dress but then became sick and was not able to participate.

Although Maria appears to be depressed and not highly motivated, she will sometimes think about her future. At one point she expressed that she wanted to become a doctor. She looks at her future as being scary. She typically wants to stay at home where she feels the most safe but is socially isolated. She has a great deal of social anxiety which was most likely worsened when she was not allowed to participate in graduation activities with her peers.

    Miss Sandy has implied that Maria is happy, kept as safe as possible, and is educated in spite of her medical issues. Maria does not complain instead she may say, "I don't feel well.". Actually, she has maintained a good sense of humor which is right in line with her family as they all make fun of the way Maria's teacher drives. Miss Sandy had backed out of the driveway over a curb and had hit the bumper of her car. The family helped her to duct tape the bumper back onto her car. Everyone had a good laugh over that one. Miss Sandy also has a tendency to spill. She will usually have a cup of coffee during her instruction time with Maria and will invariably end up having coffee spilled on herself or surrounding papers. Maria has behaviors that can be associated with Obsessive Compulsive Disorder and is very organized. The teacher tries to use her own faults to demonstrate to Maria that there is no one way to do things and the if she can accomplish a specific task so can Maria. Learning and risk taking can be fun!

Over the years the family has come to embrace Miss Sandy not only as someone who is able to help them navigate through the special education process but also through the school district policies toward those students with significant medical issues impacting educational progress. As is with many exceptional education teachers, Miss Sandy has taken on the role of advocate for her students.

It is not often that Maria ventures outside of her home where she is comfortable and is able to "shine". Off and on over the years one of her treatments has been the use of steroids. These have made her appear puffy. This in addition to other issues contribute to her shyness.

When Miss Sandy was asked what she felt Maria has brought to her life, her response was enlightening. She said that people need people to help them navigate their life especially when there are issues which impede progress. Maria demonstrated to her teacher how much we need each other. Her experience with Maria not only reinforced that it is okay to rely on others to get through life but has also been very rewarding and humbling. Her experiences with Maria "Makes me feel grateful that I have had the opportunity to help others."

Maria, like so many of the angels, comes with special gifts to those around her. She has given her family and teacher a sense of purpose in helping her to live and be successful in school. She has reinforced for the teacher that she has the abilities to teach challenging students and help them to become successful. She reinforced to her teacher that hard work can be rewarded by another's progress. She has taught all of those she knows that when freed of everyone's preconceived expectations others are able to soar demonstrating great abilities.

"Sometimes the littlest things take up the most room in your heart."

Unknown

Chapter Six
Sam's Chapter

"A babe in the house is a well-spring of pleasure, a messenger of peace and love, a resting place for innocence on earth, a link between angels and men."

Martin Farquhar Tupper *(Martin was an English writer and poet.)*

    I met Sam during one of my first years working with preschool age children with varying abilities. Sam was actually a toddler sibling to a preschool aged brother. Although I lost track of the family shortly after Sam's brother graduated from our preschool program, I still have a vivid picture of the two brothers and their mother. Our preschool was designed to serve children demonstrating difficult behaviors and help lend support to their families. Charlie, Sam's older brother, had been diagnosed with Attention Deficit Hyperactivity Disorder and Developmental Delays.

The two brothers lived with their young mother while father was spending some time in prison. Although Sam's mother, Carrie, worked hard to care for her two sons, her own personal care and parenting skills were rather limited and a bit challenging for her. Making good choices was difficult for her. Part of the agreement of being in the preschool special education program was that she participates in weekly family therapy sessions. Carrie was not only a willing participant but a very enthusiastic one as well. She looked forward to learning new skills for interacting with her sons, using new behavior management techniques in the home, and making better choices for herself and her sons. Eventually and, after the death of her young son, with the help of the family therapist, Carrie passed the GED assessment and soon enrolled in a nearby junior college. With help she would eventually pass the GED and enroll in a nearby junior college.

Prior to Carrie entering college there was an accident in the home which ended in the bathtub drowning of her youngest son, Sam. He was not yet two years old. As in many cases, the first responders were amazing. The paramedics did all they could to revive Sam however, they were unsuccessful. The first responders had seen that the mother had no resources or family support to help with the expenses of a funeral. The firefighters who had come to the home in response to the 911 call for Sam all pitched in and paid for his services and burial.

This Angel's story has been a part of my life for more than 30
years. Looking back, particularly for Sam's mother, I see all of the resiliency and strength that she demonstrated. Carrie definitely had not begun her life's journey with this strength. Her young sons had unknowingly inspired their mom to go forward even when life may hand out many challenges. Although deeply saddened by the death of Sam, Carrie was able to reach out and obtain the appropriate support for herself and her surviving son.

Sam lived among us for a short time. The impact of his life as well as his death has given myself and hopefully many others the strength to make the necessary changes to go forward productively in their own lives.

"Angels help you pick up the necessary pieces of your life and leave the rest behind."

Unknown

Chapter Seven
Jenifer's Chapter
July 11, 1971/July 13, 1971

"When you are sorrowful look again in your heart, and you shall see that in truth you are weeping for that which has been your delight."

Kahlil Gibron (Kahlil was a Lebanese-American writer, poet, visual artist, and Syrian nationalist. One of the books he is famous for is "The Prophet".)

    Approximately 45 years ago there was a couple who had been married at that time for close to twenty-five years. They had a family which included six children: Sherri, Cindy, Gary, Greg, Mike, and Pete. The youngest of these children, Pete, was 18 years of age. Mike, who is the next oldest son, and Pete were living in the home with their parents during the pregnancy and birth.

The parents were both in their early 40's. Unknown to them, the woman began having some difficulties in the area of her female reproductive region. After a visit to the doctor, a "dilation and curettage", more commonly known as a D&C, was performed. This procedure is to dilate the cervix and uterine lining and is performed for a variety of medical reasons. Soon after the procedure, it was determined that she was actually pregnant. The couple switched doctors immediately. During the pregnancy the mother developed high blood pressure.

The father had a premonition that he would need to make a choice between the mother and the baby. He spoke with his wife and informed her of his premonition and told her that if forced to make a decision, he would choose to save the baby. Mike recalls that his mother, recognizing that her husband was "in a mood", had no visible reaction to his choice.

Mike and his older brother Gary share the same opinion that their mother would have made the same choice as their father - to save the baby. One of the factors considered in this decision was that of the mother's health at the time.

  The mother went to the hospital on July 11th in labor. The professionals examining her were considering that the baby could be in a breech position. She was given a scan 2 1/2 hours prior to delivery where it was discovered that; although there had always been one heartbeat heard during routine checkups, she actually was carrying triplets! The woman gave birth to the three babies: 2 boys and one girl, Jenifer. One boy and the girl were born on July 11th with the second boy closely following on July 12th. Shortly after the delivery it was discovered that the Jenifer had a heart defect. Angel Jenifer passed away 33 hours after birth.

  I remember talking to the father several years later about his baby girl. At that time there was not a reflection on what he had felt about her purpose in life. He was still too devastated and angry by the condition of her body after an autopsy had been performed. The father had rarely cried in his life, but this is one time that his tears flowed. Mike commented that Jenifer had revealed her father's soft side and that the twins were cherished in a different manner than their older siblings.

The parents are no longer alive to interview however, I have contemplated the purpose of her life and what impact it has made on me and my life. Based on my belief that every being has a purpose for entering into our lives, I have searched for years as to what this tiny Angel could have brought to me. One possibility that comes to mind is that Jenifer offered an avenue for which I could communicate with the parents and get some perspective into their lives and the compassionate people that they were. I have found that many times a person may seem gruff on the outside while actually harboring much sadness in their heart. I believe that this was the case with Angel Jenifer's father.

I did not know Jenifer's father prior to her birth however, it is my understanding that in his younger days he was considered as a "tough guy" and he was quite stern with his other older children. As I watched him raise his younger twin sons, I saw love, compassion, understanding, protectiveness, and guidance. This was apparently not visible with the manner in which he raised his older children. I am not sure if that was because he raised his older children modeled after the way he was raised (his father's behavior has also been described as being rather brusque with his children) and did not know how to demonstrate his love or if he ultimately came to an understanding that there was another way to raise children. Perhaps experiencing the fragility of Jenifer helped him to realize that children are a precious gift that need to be nurtured and loved.

Jenifer's father was given a second chance to raise children and did so in a completely different manner than his older sons and daughters. He was given a chance for a new start and a new opportunity for raising his younger children. The older children were frequently treated with gruffness; the parent's younger children were raised using past experiences to assist in decision making and child rearing techniques. On more than one occasion the older children have been heard to say, "That would never have been the way we were treated." (Just to clarify, it is always said in a loving manner.)

I believe in my heart that Angel Jenifer was sent to her family to be a teacher and messenger. The message; children are fragile and impressionable requiring gentleness and understanding along with love to become the best people they possibly can. Her parents and siblings seem to have gotten her message.

"When someone dies, an angel is there to meet them at the gates of Heaven to let them know that their life has just begun."

Unknown

Chapter Eight
Matthew's Chapter
December 6, 2011/January 3, 2013

"When someone you love becomes a memory, the memory becomes a treasure."

Unknown

    Robyn and her partner, Scott were living in the same household with Robyn's son Robert. During this time, Robin became pregnant with Matthew. Matthew was a beautiful baby boy born to his mother, Robyn, and his father on December 6, 2011 weighing 8lbs. 6 ounces and was 21 inches long.

Matthew's parents' lives were filled with a variety of emotions including joy as well as anguish. The pregnancy was more than a little uncomfortable for Robyn, yet she loved her baby as much as anyone can be loved.

During pregnancy Robyn did not have morning sickness. Robyn also recalls that Matthew did not move during the entire pregnancy. The due date was set at December 25th. Robyn had been seeing a chiropractor once a week as Matthew was positioned into her ribs and had actually dislocated a few. The ribs were pushed back into place and Robyn wore a band to be able to facilitate breathing. Eighteen weeks into the pregnancy Robyn had the first scan conducted. This scan indicated a typically developing baby boy with no pressure on Matthew's brain. Two weeks later contractions began, and Robyn was placed in the category of High Risk pregnancy and placed on bed rest. Her ribs being dislocated causing difficulty breathing was also a concern and part of the determining factors leading to bed rest.

All new scans were performed which took close to 2 hours. Robyn began to think that there was something wrong with her baby. Her intuition was correct. They went into the supervisor's office where they were told that there was part of

Matthew's brain missing. During the next scan, Matthew flipped into a breech position and it was detected that he had a seizure. Matthew did not usually make any movements and when he did the actions were discovered to be due to seizure activity. It was discovered that Matthew and Robyn shared the same genetic mutation. Usually shared genetic characteristics are interesting to track as the child develops. This was not the case for Robyn and Matthew. What Robyn was able to witness was a progression in deterioration of Matthew's physical health.

Matthew was born via C-Section on December 6th. For Matthew and his mother this was the beginning of a long struggle for life which ended with him moving on to begin a new life. He was originally diagnosed with agenesis of the corpus callosum and hydroencephalitis. According to rarediseases.org "Agenesis of the corpus callosum or (ACC) is a rare disorder that is present at birth (congenital). It is characterized by a partial or complete absence of an area of the brain that connects the two cerebral hemispheres." This occurs when the white matter connecting the two hemispheres of the brain does not develop normally during pregnancy.

Although not all people diagnosed with ACC

have seizures, this can be an indicator when seizures occur during the first weeks after birth or within the first two years of life. Matthew actually began having seizures in utero. As with most medical conditions there is a continuum of severity. Some people never know that they may suffer from ACC until they have reached adulthood and have experienced some sort of an incident requiring a brain scan that concludes the agenesis of the corpus callosum.

At birth Matthew's weight and length were within normal ranges with his head circumference in the 90th percentile range and his general size in the 50th percentile range. He remained in the NICU (Neonatal Intensive Care Unit) annex for about two weeks. This is where the baby is not sick enough for the NICU but is not ready to go home. During this time Robyn learned how to care for her baby boy including feeding through a gastric tube. The feeding tube was necessary as Matthew was not getting enough nourishment when feeding using a bottle. Robyn practically lived at the hospital with Matthew leaving for only short periods of time. Since Matthew never cried indicating discomfort of any sort his feeding was on a schedule.

Matthew was able to come home a few days before Christmas. Robyn had a nurse come to the home every other day for the first month. Matthew's room at home had so much equipment and supplies similar to those at the hospital that it actually resembled his room at the hospital. As parents we will do anything to keep our children safe. I know that many parents have had a similar experience to Robyn's when bringing their new baby with special medical needs home, however, it is difficult for those of us who have not this experience to imagine all of the emotions going through the minds of the parents during this time. The learning curve during the time of training how to meet the needs of an infant with medical issues is enormous. Robyn came through with all the love in her heart.

All was going well and Matthew was growing stronger as each day passed. A huge milestone was that he was showing progress eating from a bottle and was being weaned from the feeding tube. He was free from the feeding tube for about three weeks when a setback occurred. An infection had set in. Robyn took him to Phoenix Children's hospital where he was diagnosed with a respiratory infection.

Matthew's pediatrician was especially concerned for his respiratory condition. He had irregular breathing, heart rate, and chest sounds. There had been a discussion about a diagnosis of congestive heart failure. Robyn commented that Matthew spent half of his life at Phoenix Children's Hospital where the staff tried to increase his quality of life whenever they could. At one point during this time, Matthew was switched from a gravity fed feeding tube to a pump feeding tube.

Matthew had been classified as disabled. He had no muscle control, developed cataracts, and had ocular albinism. (According to eyesightwear.com, "Ocular albinism is a genetic condition that primarily affects the eyes. The condition reduces the coloring (pigmentation) of the iris, which is the colored part of the eye, and the retina, which is the light sensitive tissue at the back of the eye. Pigmentation in the eye is essential for normal vision.") He was practically albino with white hair, blues eyes, and white skin. Matthew also would have "tummy time" but rolling over did not happen. It was also discovered that Matthew had a great many allergies. (Robyn said that she has only one allergy; clams.)

Matthew had come home in January 2012. During the time frame of February to October he had developed various infections including respiratory infections. He had had cataract surgery during this period as well and was wearing glasses. He also had a variety of services including speech, physical therapy, occupation al therapy, and swallowing therapy. Robyn stated that his head was egg shaped and maybe could have used a helmet however, he did not have a helmet as it had been deemed that it would not be of any benefit. For visual tracking purposes, Matthew would use a red ball which created a visual contrast. Matthew did need to sit up rather than lay down to be comfortable. He could not be taken outside due to the ocular albinism. Although there were all of the above medical (particularly respiratory) and therapeutic issues, Matthew had not been diagnosed as terminally ill at this time. Eventually Robyn returned to work and was able to check in with hospital staff to monitor his progress throughout the day.

In October Matthew began having seizures. These were infantile seizures and were rhythmic in nature. A specialist was called and Matthew was referred to a neurologist. He was admitted to the hospital and his stay lasted for 1 1/2 months. Robyn was asked if she would sign a (DNR) Do Not Resuscitate and did so. Matthew was 10 months old and there were now enough symptoms to make an additional diagnosis of Vici Syndrome. Vici Syndrome is defined as: "a very rare and severe congenital multisystem disorder characterized by the principal features of agenesis of corpus callosum, cataracts, oculocutaneous hypopigmentation, cardiomyopathy, and combined immunodeficiency." All of these indicators/symptoms were present in Matthew's medical history. At the time of Matthew's diagnosis there were only 22 diagnosed cases in the United States. Robyn was still working at this time.

On November 2nd Matthew came home. He had 24-hour nursing care and was on many medications. He was getting no better but still had not been diagnosed as terminally ill. His formula which continued to be administered via feeding a tube was switched to Pedialight, breast milk, and nutramigen. Eventually he was on 100% Pedialight.

Matthew had come home in time to celebrate Thanksgiving. He was also able to have a big party for his 1st birthday on December 6th. Matthew's half-brother, Robert, became ill with the stomach flu and been vomiting. Two days later Matthew became ill as well and developed fever spikes. He was given ice baths but his fever would not come down. At 4:00 the next morning, Matthew was taken into hospice care at the Ryan House in Phoenix, Arizona. Robyn stopped working to spend all of her time with her one year-old son and also had Robert who was ten years old at the time with her at the Ryan House. Between the stomach bug and his current infection, Matthew was unable to recover. His medications stopped and he was given morphine in an attempt to keep him comfortable.

Matthew was admitted to the Ryan House three days after his first birthday. He remained in the loving care of his mother until his passing while in his mother's arms on January 3rd.

Robyn stated that Matthew could recognize her voice. Robyn always had music playing for him and she would sing to him. He used to talk to her; just her. She knew he loved her and he knew he was loved. The recovery of Matthew's passing has been difficult to say the least for Robyn. Matthew's story is a testament to the theory that good can come out of all situations.

Robyn and Matthew's father were never married. After Matthew was born with medical issues his father became more and more distant leaving most of his care to Robyn and medical professionals. He eventually was not there offering support in any area, physically, emotionally, or financially to either Robyn or Matthew. I have stated in a previous chapter how it is sometimes quite difficult to accept or come to terms with the aspect of having a seriously ill child. I can only imagine the many feelings that both of Matthew's parents had. As Robyn was left alone to deal with the realistic impact that Matthew's health issues had on a daily basis, I believe that she ended up a stronger and enriched person.

Matthew and his mother were very close. He gave his mother the strength to leave the current abusive relationship that she was in. Robyn is now happily married to a wonderful man who has accepted and adopted her first son, Robert. He has been a significant influence in her healing.

There are many kinds of love. There are many forms that love may take. There are many relationships that boast of the feeling of love. The love of a mother to a child is unique and unable to be duplicated. The relationship between a mother and child is as individual and unique as they are.

Matthew's mother loved him more each and every day during his time on earth and continues to this very day.

"There has to be evil so that good can prove its purity above it."

"Peace comes from within. Do not seek it without."

Buddha *(Buddha was also a monk, mendicant (beggar), and sage (wise through reflection and experience). He also is the founder of the teachings of Buddha.)*

Epilogue

- David is thriving well with only a few setbacks compared to what he has previously experienced.

- Chase continues to live and spread his smiles with all who encounter him.

- Mark is a person with a great character bring joy to the many people fortunate enough to cross his path. Hopefully in the future we may hear more about Mark.

- If all goes well for Maria she is targeted to graduate from high school in December of 2019.

The following is my personal reflection on the subject of children as Angels:

Most fortunate are we who have been chosen to have an Angel in our midst. The Angels among us love us, forgive us, calm us, and teach us.

The next time you are out and about and happen upon an angel, watch for all of the smiles and laughter of those near the angel. These smiles are with the people who embrace and take to heart all of the gifts that are presented to them.

Acknowledgments

My deepest and most sincere gratitude goes to the parents, grandparents, family members, foster parents, guardians, educators, therapists, medical staff and a score of others who have been a part of giving our angels the highest quality of life available. Thank you to all who entrusted me with their thoughts and feelings concerning the Angel that has been part of their lives and continues to enrich and improve the quality of their lives.

About the Author

Ruth Ann was born in Waukegan, Ill. She knew from as early age that she wanted to help those people who were hearing impaired. She ultimately followed that dream in a much broader sense. She became a special education teacher and ended her official career as a Director of Exceptional Education Services. As we can see by this book, she is unable to let go of her focus on children and the many gifts that they bring to this world as well as the belief that everyone has a purpose in life.

*A portion of the proceeds will go to benefit children with special needs.

Made in the USA
San Bernardino, CA
05 November 2019